MY MILITARY BROKE-ASSNESS:

A Book on Finance Written by a Broke-Ass E-5

By

VIC...

Vision, Initiative, Courage

Charleston, SC
www.PalmettoPublishing.com

My Military Brokeassness
Copyright © 2022 by VIC…Vision, Initiative, Courage

Hardcover ISBN: 979-8-8229-0267-1
Paperback ISBN: 979-8-88590-596-1
Ebook ISBN: 979-8-88590-597-8

To all service members—past, present, and future—
thank you for all that you do.

Civilians, I highly encourage you to read this book.

To all the Karens of the world, if this book offends
you, then fuck you, and whatever the male version of a
Karen is, fuck you too.

INTRODUCTION

As a ten-year active-duty veteran, one thing I've noticed while serving is the inadequate information we receive about basic finances. Usually, our punk-ass "leaders" tell us to be mentally, physically, emotionally, and spiritually ready to fight. However, rarely do they tell us to be financially fit. In my opinion the reason they don't is that their shit is fucked up too. So I've provided a useful tool to help bring some clarity and a bit of direction to help you become financially sound. With that being said, let's jump in, have a good time, and learn some shit.

Army: This book is short and easy to understand. Don't worry, my ASVAB score was low as shit too.

Marines: If you turn to the end of the book, you'll find two blank pages to color on. Crayons not included.

Air Force: Your fat asses should be able to finish this book in a day while sitting at your desk, most likely not doing shit.

Navy: I'm sorry, this is a book on finance. No love stories or gay shit here.

Coast Guard: No comment. Nobody cares about you.

CHAPTER 1

FINANCIAL BEHAVIOR

We all deal with money in some way, shape, or form. The thing is how you go about it is up to you. Most of the time, personal finances are based off our financial behavior. Usually, we buy shit because we want it and don't need it. By having the ability to be aware and mitigate empty expenditures, you'll save more money. This requires some focus and discipline to achieve, not just short term but definitely long term as well. Even today from time to time, I impulse-buy shit I don't need; however, I'm aware of it, and I've developed the following small methods to better help my spending habits:

1. Carry cash.

2. Develop a budget.

3. Make a list.

4. Eat home-cooked meals/meal prep.

5. Leave all cards and cash at home.

All these are proven methods that will help you slow down or even stop empty expenses and leave you with more money in your pocket.

Cash Only

By carrying cash, it cuts down on the use of your debit and credit card purchases. When we use our cards, we're more inclined to spend more money. Also, when using cash, not only does it help save money, but studies have shown that it also gives off small pain receptors in the brain. With a debit card, not only are you getting the product but you also get your card back. So naturally, you spend more. But with cash it hurts. Next time carry some cash and spend $100 and see how it feels.

Develop a Budget

Having a budget and sticking to it will help save more money. One thing I've noticed when talking with some of the so-called professionals on base is that they say "stick to the budget" but don't give any example how. In a later chapter, I will share types of budgeting methods.

Make a List

When going to the commissary, grocery store, or wherever the fuck you shop, have a list. Again, this will help you stay focused and disciplined when making purchases. To really challenge yourself, carry cash too to help stop you from buying Coca-Cola and Oreo cookies because we all know your fat ass doesn't need it.

Home-Cooked Meals

I get it; after a long-ass day at work, we're tired as shit. The last thing we want to do is cook. I know, you have to decide what to cook, prep it, and then clean up afterward. The way I see it, it will help save some money, but let's be real; again, the last thing you need is McDonald's or Burger King. Sometimes you can't have it your way.

Meal Prep

I remember when I was an even broker E-3, there would be months where I checked my bank statement and had repeatedly eaten fast food. On average I was spending $300 a month. Mind you, at this time I was single, lived on base, and had meal card access. Luckily, it was my superior genetics that've kept me looking good. Just imagine where I would be today if I saved that money over time. Still broke-ass fuck.

Leave All Cards and Cash at Home

If you're really struggling and the meal prepping or budgeting isn't working, then you just fucking suck. You're a fucking failure at life, and nobody likes you. The last thing to do is just fucking kill yourself. No, please don't fucking kill yourself. Obviously, you have to take drastic measures.

Leave all your cash and cards at home until you can gain that focus and discipline. But still, nobody likes you.

What Works for You

Develop your own method. Have your own strategy and plan laid out the way you want it. Just remember to stay focused and disciplined. If it works, don't keep it to yourself; share it with others so they can put themselves in a better financial situation as well.

CHAPTER 2

CUT THE BULLSHIT

A lot of the time, we know we're fucked up financially but don't know how and where to start. Well, in order to start, you have to be real with yourself and start by listing all your expenses, then cut down the bullshit. It's not going to be easy, but it's going to help. For example, how many streaming services do you have—Netflix, Hulu, or Disney+? How many phone app services do you have—YouTube Premium, Spotify, or Amazon Prime? All I'm trying to tell you is that this shit adds up to big numbers monthly, then annually.

Let's Cut Some Shit

- Cable—who the fuck watches TV anyways?

- Streaming services

- Phone app services

- Online subscriptions

- Smartphone plan

- Any other reoccurring monthly expenses (Pornhub Premium, gym memberships, etc.)

These things listed above are nothing but wants. Now if you're smart, just borrow someone else's Netflix or Hulu account and chill. See what I did there?

Needs versus Wants

Obviously, we all have needs. Gotta pay the bills, buy groceries, and make sure our cars are covered. These are all examples of needs. Even with needs there are still ways to cut cost. For example, perhaps walk to work a few times a week, take a bike, or carpool to cut gas usage or turn off all the lights in rooms nobody is using.

We also have wants, like that cup of coffee or perhaps the latest trend item we wanted but not necessary. This right here is just another example of financial behavior. And yes, I'm going to be using this term a lot, so fuck you. In the end how far you want to change your financial decision-making is up to you. However, with a good, sound budget, you can have your cake and eat it too.

CHAPTER 3

A SOUND BUDGET

A budget is simply a tool used to see where your money is going, whether it be weekly, monthly, or annually. In this chapter we'll be discussing different types of budgets available and which method I use.

50-30-20 Budget
This budget is based off a monthly basis.

Fifty percent of your income goes to needs:

- Food

- Housing

- Utilities

- Insurance

- Transportation

- Child Care

- Alcohol (Yes, it is a motherfuckin' need.)

Thirty percent of your income goes to wants:

- Entertainment

- Dining out

- Reoccurring monthly subscriptions

- Shopping

- Drugs

Twenty percent of your income goes to savings and debt:

- Debt

- Savings account

- Thrift Savings Plan (TSP)/401(k)

70-20-10 Budget

This budget is based off a monthly basis.

Seventy percent of your income goes to needs and wants:

- Food

- Housing

- Utilities

- Insurance

- Transportation

- Child care

- Entertainment

- Dining out

- Reoccurring monthly subscriptions

- Shopping

- Alcohol and drugs

Twenty percent of your income goes to savings and debt:

- Debt

- Savings account

Ten percent of your income goes to wherever the fuck you want:

- Investment

- College fund

- Donation

- More drugs

The budgets mentioned above can change based on your financial situation, but they do work as long you're willing to put in a little fucking effort. Listed below is the type of budget I use, plus some other factors.

Envelope Budget

I use the envelope budget. This does require discipline and focus. After all bills and expenses have come out (electric, water, etc.), I must physically go to the bank and withdraw cash. This is where I must really do my due diligence and calculate how money I need to fill the envelopes. For example, I'll withdraw $400 cash.

- Gas - $75

- Grocery - $200

- Entertainment - $75

- Miscellaneous - $50

The total is $400. Because we get paid on the first and fifteenth of the month—yes, this is biweekly—that means this money must last me almost two weeks, sometimes longer depending on the pay period. Any money that has been taken from the envelope I must annotate and subtract from the money inside. Any money left in the envelopes either at the end of the pay period or end of the month I can choose to keep in the residing envelope, or I can reward myself and move it over to a different one.

This budget works effectively for myself. I'm able to track every dollar I spend while still be able to enjoy life while staying in control of my expenses. For the remaining money in my checking account, I can choose to either save it, invest it, or pay off debt. The number of envelopes you want to utilize is up to you.

CHAPTER 4

MY CAR

Let's be honest, we love our fucking car. We love our cars more than our badass kids, more than our wives, and sometimes more than ourselves. We love our cars, especially in the military. Guys, we love our cars so much that we'll overcompensate because of our small dicks and buy a big-ass, gas-guzzling V-8 Camaro, Charger, Challenger, or Mustang. Ladies, you love looking good in your car too. That nice Acura, Mercedes, or Lexus makes you look sleek and sexy while taking a photo of yourself and posting it to Instahoes—I mean, Instagram.

Does Your Car Love You?

Yep, we all love our cars. The question is, does that car love you back? Does that 15 percent interest rate or higher, plus insurance, ensure you that car is for you? Can you truly afford it right now? Do you love having that high car payment as well? And it's not like the term limit on the car is short too. You most likely financed it for seventy-two months or, in some circumstances, longer. If this is you, don't worry, I did it once too.

Back when I was a broke-ass E-3, I had just gotten to my new base. Mind you, I had no debt; I was twenty-two years old, just starting life on my own. From my living quarters to my workplace was probably two to three miles. I don't really remember; that was over ten years ago. Obviously, I didn't have a car and felt pressured to buy one because I had to keep asking coworkers to pick me up and drop me off, plus going to lunch. Also, I didn't want to be confined to base the whole time, so I said "Fuck it," went out, and purchased a car.

Because I wasn't overcompensating and didn't want to get killed by gas prices, I did take somewhat of a logical approach to my vehicle purchase. I ended up buying a brand-new Nissan Sentra at sticker price. The car payment was $400, plus insurance at $125 a month. The term limit was seventy-two months with an interest rate of 10 percent. Looking back, it took me seven years to pay off that shitty car—seven years because of refinance. Although like I said before I may not have been overcompensating, I did get tentacled.

Don't Get Tentacled by Dealerships

Right now you're probably asking yourself, "What the fuck does *tentacled* mean?" Have you ever watched a Japanese anime porn where the girl goes into a room, and behind another door or closet comes out this big-ass monster or machine with all these tentacles, and it starts juicing her holes (mouth, ass, pussy)? That's called being tentacled, and car dealerships are fucking notorious for doing this to people, especially the unaware or uneducated.

I once worked with a young lady who at the time was nineteen years old, nice girl, big-ass titties. Anyways, me being a broke E-5 and her an even broker E-3, I inquired about her car note. We called the bank who financed her, and they said, "Your car payment is $330 a month with a 24 percent interest rate." This young lady wasn't just being tentacled, but they were taking her life force too. I worked with her, and she ended up refinancing to 11 percent, which is a shitload better but not good. Below I'm going to give advice on how to purchase a car and what to look for so you don't get tentacled.

Private Seller

I've purchased four vehicles in my life so far, one from a dealership, others from a private seller. The vehicles I've purchased via private seller were my favorites. To start with, you get the vehicles a lot cheaper. The same vehicle at a dealership probably would've been marked up way more, plus fees. With a private seller, there is no hassle, just you and the seller deciding on a price. The only negatives are warranty and vehicle condition. That why it's imperative to take it to a registered mechanic for inspection to make sure you're not purchasing a piece of shit. And it happens. A good friend of mine made a $15,000 mistake. Stupid-ass E-4.

The YOLO Approach

Everyone does it at some point when purchasing a vehicle. They go with the YOLO approach. I see this all the time; the mindset is "I'm young, I look good, and I could die tomorrow, so I might as well live my life to the fullest. YOLO!" To the unaware or uneducated, *YOLO* means "you only live once." Although true, this is the dumbest goddamn thing you can do. You fucking idiot, by doing this, you put yourself in financial hardship and massive debt with some car that is going to depreciate faster than the thirty-year-old hot chick chasing down a young NBA player. Nobody should be using this method to purchase a vehicle unless you absolutely enjoy being tentacled.

Delayed Gratification

Simply put, delayed gratification is where you reward yourself by saving money now and making a big purchase later. So if your number is $5,000 or $15,000, you'll just save up to buy the car you want later. Personally, I've rarely seen this method being used. Who the hell has that kind of patience, especially with these little punk-ass paychecks we receive? However, if you have the focus and discipline, perhaps this method is for you.

The Beater

This is where you have the smart "fuck it, I don't care how I look" approach. This is where you'll purchase a car for $1,500 just to get from A to B. In a way this could tie into delayed gratification. But if you don't care about upgrading, just keep saving and investing your money. Good job, you fucking nerd.

20-4-10 Rule

This is the method I use. Basically, the 20-4-10 rule is a 20 percent down payment on a car. For example, 20 percent of $20,000 is $4,000, followed by a term limit of four years or forty-eight months, followed by 10 percent of your monthly income. So the remaining car note is $16,000 with a car payment of $333 plus interest. Now if your monthly take-home is $3,000, that means your car payment should be around $300 a month. By using this method, it means you pay your car off faster, and you do your due diligence to see how much your car payment is going to be. Don't forget maintenance and insurance.

Bank versus Credit Union

Before even walking into a dealership or looking at purchasing a vehicle, be sure to get preapproved from your bank or credit union. This gives you all the control and alleviates stress. If your bank gives you a higher interest rate, try going to a credit union. Historically, credit unions have lower interest rates than banks.

Mad AF

Recently, my unit acquired a brand-new member—a young, broke-ass E-2 probably around nineteen or twenty years of age, no family, single, and lives on post. There I am, sitting at my desk, trying to get some work done for once, when a member of my "leadership" walks in, this stupid-ass O-2. At this time the young man (E-2) was being assisted by an E-4, just showing him the ropes and doing some training. The typical questions asked were "Where are you from?" and shit like that. Then the lieutenant asked, "Do you have a vehicle?"

The young E-2 responded, "No, sir."

The answer out of the lieutenant's mouth was "You should probably get one." He said bye to everyone, then walked out of the office. No fucking context at all, no tips, no financial advice, and he didn't even direct him to on-base financial agencies to help establish some type of budget.

I don't know why, but in that moment, I got so fucking pissed. I get it; nobody is going to babysit him. Got to get to work on time, go to appointments, and avoid the weather. I really wanted to find that lieutenant and slap the shit out of him for that dumbass answer, but for now I still needed this job, maybe later. One reason I probably got so mad was that I saw myself in that same situation—I didn't know shit, and it cost me a lot of money later.

And this is where the trickle-down effect could occur. He's most likely going to buy a car he can barely afford and with a high interest rate because of lack of credit history. He's young, so his insurance is going to be priced out the ass, plus gas and maintenance, all while accruing massive debt. This is the start of potential financial hardship.

Don't Feel Pressured

Don't feel pressured into purchasing a vehicle. I'm just speaking from experience. Here I was, first time in the real world, young as hell, don't know shit, depending on others to get me around but with zero debt. When I purchased my first vehicle, I got tentacled. I didn't take any of these factors into account—insurance, car payment, gas, maintenance, interest rate, and length of loan term. It took me years to pay that car off. I share this with you all so you don't make my mistakes. Be patient; if you have to walk, then walk or buy a bike or borrow rides. Fuck it. If people or even your leadership gives you a hard time because you don't have a car, fuck them; it's your life. Do what you have to do until you're in a financially stable position to purchase a vehicle. Also, if you see someone walking on base, offer them a ride. Don't be a dick.

CHAPTER 5

DEBT

We all have debt. Hell, the entire global financial system is based on debt. So technically, if you're not borrowing money, you aren't doing right, although, of course, it all depends on how much you borrow and how well you maintain it. Also, the type of debt you have goes a long way too.

Types of Debts

There are many types of debts. They are

- auto loans,

- credit card debt,

- student loans,

- home loans, and

- personal loans.

These are also known as consumer debt. We are the consumer, and we are what makes the economy run. However, sometimes we get so far up shit creek that we allow it to consume us and start making irrational, dumbass decisions.

Irrational, Dumbass Decisions

Deep down you know who you are, making dumbass, brash decisions, getting into massive debt because of a car you can't afford and with a high-ass interest rate. What's more fucked up is the piece-of-shit-ass car dealership knows it but still allows you to drive off the car lot. Anyways, this is just another part of being a good, conscientious financial decision maker and a good financial behavior. Don't buy shit you know your dumb ass can't afford.

Not All Debt Is Bad

It is what it is; sometimes we have to borrow money to sustain our livelihood. For example, if you wanted to buy a house for $200,000, chances are you won't have that kind of money sitting around, so the other alternative is to borrow, or what if you have a family and can't take a risk on buying a crap car? You're probably going to borrow again to find something reliable, safe, and affordable. This is where making sound financial decisions comes in. Take all variables into effect like your annual income, monthly income, expenses, budget, and any other financial obligations you may have. This is where you are in control of your finances and can definitely take some debt on because it's necessary.

Getting Rid of Debt

Getting rid of debt fucking sucks; trust me, I know personally. I would rather have taken that lump sum of cash and use it elsewhere. But I knew I wanted this debt monster off my ass so I can have peace of mind and not be stressed out. This process takes time, but again, it comes back to focus and discipline, unless you continually want to be a slave to debt. The best way to get rid of debt is to just start paying that shit off quickly and efficiently. There are number of different ways to start paying off your debts.

- Create a side hustle/Second job

- Borrow from friends and family

- Create an allotment

- Crowdfunding

- Play the lottery/Gamble

- Sell that ass

Got to do what you got to do. These are just a few examples. Personally, I started with the highest interest rate first regardless of the loan amount. The thing is just to start; this process may not work for you, but just start and get rid of your debt. If you have too many debts and can't keep tract, consider doing a debt consolidation.

Debt Consolidation

In a consolidation the bank will grant you a personal loan for the amounts of remaining debts you have and allow you to pay them off with one lump sum. The only drawback is you still have debt, but now it is just one loan. Take into consideration the interest rates other debts may have; usually, personal loans have higher interest rates.

Borrowing from Your TSP

Yes, this is an option. Many so-called experts may not agree with you in regard to borrowing from your retirement fund because they say you're messing with your future. To them I say, "Fuck off." It's your life; why wait thirty or forty years to use your own money? Better your situation now, and get that debt monster off your ass. Learn from your mistakes and move on. Plus, the way I see it, after paying off the debt, you'll still have more money to contribute to your TSP/401(k), so it's a win-win.

CHAPTER 6

CREDIT

We've all seen those goofy-ass, fast-paced commercials where they're trying to sell you a car. "Good credit, bad credit, no credit, no problem. If you have $500 and a job, we'll get you in a car today." Meanwhile, you go down to car dealership Tentacles 'R' Us, and it's just a bunch of bullshit. The question is, what is credit? How come having credit has to play such a big role in our financial decision-making? I'll tell you why—because, again, it's a bunch of bullshit yet kind of necessary.

What Is Credit?

Credit is the ability to borrow money with an agreement to pay back at a later time—to pay back, not skip or forget payments. Credit also allows you to build up your credit score and credit history as well as your FICO score.

Establishing Credit

There are plenty of ways to establish your credit. Perhaps secure a credit card. This is where you make a deposit into an account as a safeguard, just in case you miss a payment—a reasonable car payment. Hell, you can get a Military Star card; just don't fuck up like I did—miss your payments for months and end up in front of the commander. I was just irresponsible as fuck. Dumbass E-3 I was.

The Credit Card

With great power comes great responsibility. Ah yes, the credit card, possibly one of the greatest or worst inventions created by the banking system, of course depending on how you use it. It can be used as a tool to help build and establish your credit while receiving rewards. On the other hand, it could lead to self-destruction instead. There are thousands of different credit card plans and offers available, all with different types of incentives.

Credit Score

Your credit score is a three-digit number between 300 and 850; it's used to determine how well you repay your debts based on credit history. The higher the score, the lower the interest rates; plus, it allows you be to more eligible to receive more financial opportunities. Here's a look into how your credit score is computed:

300–500: Very poor to deep subprime

501–600: Poor to subprime

601–660: Fair to nonprime

661–780: Good to prime

781–850: Excellent to superprime

Not only does your credit score determine your financial history and behavior, but it also determines how responsible you are. For instance—some of you may have been too young to remember or perhaps were a cause of it—back in 2008 the United States suffered a massive real estate collapse. One of the biggest reasons was that dumbass banks were lending to people with subprime credit history. So these financially irresponsible people were receiving a mortgage along with a high interest rate; an assload of people defaulted on their mortgages, like, what the fuck do you think was going to happen?

Another reason to maintain your credit history is to get a job; yes, big corporations and companies will do a credit report/check on you to see if you keep your shit in check. Also, it's to make sure you're not a threat, subject to extortion or bribery. This is a reason why we have to do that piece-of-shit cyber awareness training modules every year. Thanks, Hilary!

FICO Score

FICO stands for Fair Isaac Corporation. Lenders use borrowers' FICO score and other factors to determine risk and credit line. Your FICO score is composed of the following five parts:

- 35 percent payment history

- 30 percent amounts owed

- 15 percent length of credit history

- 10 percent credit mix

- 10 percent new credit

Both your credit and FICO scores report and retrieve your information from the following three bureaus:

- Equifax

- Experian

- TransUnion

All are responsible for collecting and maintaining consumer credit reports in the United States. These reports are then provided to subscribers, such as landlords, mortgage lenders, credit card companies, and others who are deciding whether to extend you credit.

CHAPTER 7

THE MARRIAGE LIFE

Since being in the military for ten years and counting, I've seen some shit, and I imagine a lot of you are the same. But when it comes to marriage in the military, the only questions I ask is, *What the fuck?* Having been deployed several times and stationed overseas, people are crazy, with married people actually being the worst. I'm not going to get into specifics, but I could probably write a book on that alone. Y'all nasty.

Before Marriage

Whether you're military or civilian, if you're going to get married anytime soon, congratulations. Piece of advice: don't do it. Anyways, this is where communication must come in play, especially financially because once you allow your finances to go in disarray, everything else from here on out goes on a downward spiral that could eventually end your marriage or worse. Establish a game plan for any unpaid debts, gambling habits, or even if you're supporting family here or abroad. Having this conversation

27

before putting a ring on it is detrimental. I'm only speaking from experience.

The BMW

Gentlemen, please do me a favor. Look to your left, then look to your right, or perhaps look straight in front of you. That is known as the BMW, big military wife. Its origins are unknown, but scientists have discovered that if you have one of these self-destructing, ticking time bombs, it's time to throw that big-ass beluga back into the ocean where you found her. Now understand this is what truly defines one. She doesn't work, your child is dirty as fuck, his/her diaper is leaving a trail in the carpet while they walk, the house is fucking disgusting, and she always threatening to talk to your first sergeant, and somehow while all this is going on, your bank account is being depleted of its funds. You work all day for the ten punk-ass bosses asking for the same damn shit. Get rid of it! The last thing you need is undue stress when you come home. The worst part is the pussy is not even good, like throwing a hot dog down the hallway.

Base Dwellers

Yes, we know who you are, the base dweller. You live on base. So that means all expenses are paid. No mortgage, no electric or water bill. You have access to commissary and a tax-free (Base Exchange/Post Exchange) BX/PX. Ask yourself, "Why am I always broke, and where is my money going?" For the most part, this goes all the way back to financial behavior. What's your excuse? Pull your head out of your ass and get your shit together.

Individual or Joint Bank Account

To me this decision is based on each party's financial behavior. If both parties are financially sound, then combine finances. If not, keep that shit separate. I've seen situations where finances were separate, but things were able to work out fine. They just divided the bills evenly. At the end of day, whatever works best is up to you.

Empowerment

Ladies, what's up? How are you all doing? By now you're probably thinking I hate all women. Not true, just the fat ones like Rosie O'Donnell. Hey, my commander in chief said it, so why can't I? I heard this comment before from a woman I used to work with. She said, "Oh, I don't take care of the bills and finances. I let my husband do all that."

To be honest, when she said that, my jaw dropped, and I was just thinking, What a stupid-ass comment. I mean, I guess it worked for her, but then I asked, "Is your husband a financial adviser or analyst?" Her response was no. Now I'm not saying that her husband didn't take care of her, but to me this is risky for many different reasons. As stated before, her husband wasn't a financial adviser or analyst, so how the hell would you truly know how your money is being managed? Or what if there are issues in the marriage and he was slowly stashing away cash for a rainy day? All I'm trying to say is get involved.

I've deployed not too long ago, and my wife said, "Babe, I'm bored. I miss you. I have nothing to do." I just told her to better herself. Learn, work out, go to school, find a hobby, or increase your skills. Whether your husband, wife, or transformer is here or abroad, this is where you take that time to excel. For example, plant a garden. Not only are you growing fresh fruit and veggies, but this will also allow you to have something to do. Plus, this allows you to eat better, which means save more money, and perhaps this could lead to a side hustle that could bring in more revenue, which could lead to bigger and better opportunities. Or perhaps go through the house and have a garage sale or sell things online. Take this time to learn a skill or find your passion. On the other hand, if you happen to be physically attractive, don't forget, there's always OnlyFans. I know I've been talking shit, but I love y'all. Never forget, "you is kind, you is smart, and you is important."

Divorce

In the military, divorce runs rampant like a pandemic; yeah, I went there. There were many reasons why—long work hours, deployments, infidelity, and money. As a matter of fact, money is just the trigger as to why most marriages fail. It's crazy when you truly think about how a little piece of green paper or some numbers on a screen can cause so much motherfucking sorrow. However, again, this comes back to financial behavior, communication, and living within your means. Unless you're getting your ass kicked, then you might want to leave.

CHAPTER 8

ALCOHOL ABUSE, DOMESTIC VIOLENCE, AND SUICIDE

Having been in the military for ten years, you see some shit. The good, the bad, and the ugly. And it's always the bad and ugly times you remember the most or at least think about from time to time. Being in the military is extremely stressful, sometimes damn near overwhelming. Luckily for me I've also had some type of out—good friends, exercise, and the mindset to channel any anger, pain, and frustration and try to do something constructive so I don't blow my fucking top. But many others are not so fortunate.

Alcohol

Sometimes after a long-ass day, there's nothing better than a nice, chilled Jack and Coke. Ah yes, I can taste the bubbles. Anyways, alcohol in the military is nothing but another day. Don't believe me? Check out the class six or a shopette on a Friday; that line is long as fuck. I can't tell you how many times I heard the expression "Bro, I got so fucked up this weekend." To be honest, when I wasn't even in a year yet, my commander had a bottle of Jack on heri desk so the precedence of alcohol was normalized. Yet why do we have so many issues?

Alcohol Abuse

Something that I've learned about finances is they can make or break you. If you find yourself in a situation, are you going to allow it to consume you, or are you going to overcome and kick that shit in the dick? I've seen how shitty financial behavior can tear a person apart. Alcohol isn't the answer. It'll make you feel good temporarily, but when you come out of that deep, dark state, you still have to deal with reality. Put the bottle down.

Domestic Violence

Chances are if you got slapped across the face, you probably deserved it. Next time shut the hell up. By now you've probably gotten use to my twisted sense of humor, although this shit does happen. At this point you're jeopardizing your freedom.

A coworker of mine did have issues with domestic violence. Now I'm not sure if his issues spewed from finances or his crazy-ass wife, but the military was swift as fuck and kicked his ass out; however, the court fees, because this was an off-base incident, rose to around $9,000. You thought you had financial problems now. Go ahead and start fucking with that judicial system; you'll be more fucked up than Bill Cosby's dates.

Suicide

I've experienced two suicides during my tenure in the military so far. Like I said, so far. To be honest I expect more to happen not because I'm evil or some shit like that but because now we have this sick-ass cancel culture, and we have to watch what we say and walk on eggshells. In other words our society is turning everyone, generally the younger generation, into some bitches. No backbone and lacked resiliency. Now anybody at any age can suffer from depression and financial issues. Trust me when I say that I've been down and had financial problems at the same time, but it never once appeared to me to hurt myself.

Here's a fucking solution. Don't kill yourself. For the two suicides I've experienced, one of them hit close as hell. As a matter of fact, for a short period, I was this person's boss. You would've never thought this person would take their life, but it happens. It destroyed so many lives—that of their parents, friends, spouses, coworkers, and children. And nothing was left behind but a bunch of "What happened?" and what-ifs. Suicide is never fucking the answer.

We All Struggle

The struggle is fucking real; trust me, it's real. Let me explain. There was a period in my life where I felt like a loser, inadequate, and nothing was going my way no matter how hard I tried. Work was ass, I was out of shape, my body was breaking down, I was broke as fuck, I had a massive debt, a child was on the way, I was depressed as hell, and there were marriage problems all at the same time. I was fucking struggling, and nobody knew.

However, one day I just realized how fucked up everything in my life was and noticed I had to make a change. I needed to make a change not for my family or work but for myself. And this wasn't just some overnight process; it took weeks to grow and get better. Even now as I write this, I have my moments, but during my struggles, not one fucking time did it appeal to me to hit my wife, consume alcohol, or consider taking my own life. Remember, we all got problems and issues; how you deal with them is what truly defines if you're a bitch or a fucking legend.

Be Legendary

I know it's easier said than done, but speaking up if you're having issues—whether it be mentally, emotionally, or financially—is fucking legendary. Yeah, people may be mad or disappointed, but at least they can point you in the direction to get help. Killing yourself makes you nothing but a bitch—a straight-up baby back bitch. You're fucking worth it. Life is short as fuck, and these moments of sorrow and grief shall pass. Remember, we're a team. We've got your back. Speak up, get help, and be fucking legendary.

CHAPTER 9

LIVING OFF BASE AND ABROAD

Finally, you no longer have to live on post either because of your rank, time in service, or perhaps marriage. Let's do a run-through of all the great things to expect when residing off post.

Apartments

This is usually the first option many people go for when they are finally able to live off base, a nice apartment. Makes sense. It's clean, it's quiet, and it's all yours. And the rent is usually in the confines of your basic allowance for housing. So it looks affordable. Let's see what other expenses and amenities have to be accounted for.

- Deposit for incidentals

- Internet for Pornhub

- Power to charge your phone so you can watch Pornhub

- Cable (Who watches TV?)

- Appliances (Some places don't have washer and dryers.)

- Water to wash your ass

- Pet fees (You have to pay extra to have a pet.)

- Insurance to protect your shit

As you can see, there's a lot to think about when renting an apartment. Now in some circumstances, water, power, and other amenities are already accounted for in your rent. By no means is this to discourage you from getting a place, just bringing some attention and awareness. Something to think about, that's all. At least you'll have that nice gym and swimming pool.

Get a Roommate

Now if you're thinking, I don't want a place to myself yet, or It's going to be expensive, a great option is to have a roommate. Whether they're military or civilian, having a roommate is a great way to split the bills. Whoever your roommate is, make sure that each of you has a clear understanding of when the bills need to get paid. The last thing you need is issues where you eat, sleep, and shit. One more great thing about a roommate is it helps you cut cost and save a lot of money.

Renting a House

I'm not going to get too deep into renting a house. A lot of the same issues apply as if you are getting an apartment except that, rather than dealing with apartment management, you're dealing with a landlord, who owns the property, or a property manager.

Overseas

One of the reasons we join the military is to travel right. Having the opportunity to be positioned in Germany was amazing—really clean, green as hell, and a lot to do. However, that doesn't mean it doesn't come with some financial issues. Now I can only speak from my experience in Germany. I'm not sure on how other nations regulate.

Contracts

Everything in Germany was a contract, from your phone plan to the internet and cable. Just annoying as hell. Before I came back to the United States, I had a quick turnaround from when I received my orders to my date eligible for return from overseas. Overseas doesn't acknowledge the military clause, so in essence, if you have a (Permanent Change of Station) PCS quickly to a different duty station, you're fucked. You'll still be paying on those contracts up until at least ninety days after you leave. By the way that's in euro. Also, slow the fuck down; there are speed cameras all over that damn country. Just nickel and dime the fuck out of you. But hey, that's what you get when you're a socialist nation, and nobody fucking works.

Save Your COLA

No, not Coca-Cola, you stupid-ass civilians. The overseas cost-of-living allowance (COLA) is a nontaxable allowance designed to offset the higher overseas prices of non-housing goods and services. If you're overseas for one, two, three, or four years, try your best to save your COLA. Your time overseas will fly, especially if you're out and about.

Landlords

Be cognizant of greedy-ass, shady landlords here and abroad. If you're considering living in their property, walk with them and do an extensive check of every square inch. I've heard way too many stories of tenants being taken advantage of and having their deposits stolen. Don't get tentacled.

Military Clause

A military clause is a provision included in a residential lease that allows military personnel to break a lease agreement and have security deposits returned if they are called to duty or must relocate because of connected service activity. Also, it can be utilized to break contracts like internet and phone if necessary.

The American Dream

Nothing completes the American dream like owning a home. I own a big, beautiful house. To be honest it's too much house. I'm going to downgrade eventually. But I'm living the dream. Owning a home is amazing and feels good. However, shit is expensive, a lot of motherfucking expenses. Purchasing a home is the biggest financial decision you'll make in your life besides a car. It's either going to be a fifteen-year or thirty-year decision.

VA Loan

There are many different types of mortgage loans you can utilize when purchasing a home. You have Federal Housing Administration loans and conventional loan, just to name a few. For beautiful veterans like ourselves, we have the privilege to avail of the VA loan. One of the biggest advantages when using a VA loan to purchase a home is there is no down payment. Most loans have some sort of down payment, ranging from 3 percent up to 25 percent. This has a lot to do with your credit score. To apply for a VA loan, you need a minimum of a 620 score. Looks like there's hope for your broke ass after all.

Rent or Sale

In the military we are constantly being PCS'd, which brings us to the question, should I rent or sell my home? There are a lot of factors that can determine this decision—location, state, how long I have lived in the residence, ability to rent my home, and so forth. If you sell, you take your lump sum of cash and move on. Save it, pay off debt, or invest it. Out of sight, out of mind. You don't have to worry about it. If you rent, you'll have to hire a property manager, and they'll receive a small percentage of the rent, but every month you receive some money from the tenant. This is known as passive income. Who doesn't like easy money?

CHAPTER 10

FINANCIAL PREVENTION VERSUS FINANCIAL RECOVERY

Financial Prevention

Again, I always come back to behavior and discipline. Too many times I've seen and heard veterans and civilians making irrational financial decisions because they either don't care, got screwed over, or thought they could afford it. Usually, the biggest financial fuckup is cars, followed by credit card debt. Ask yourself, "Is putting myself in a fucked-up financial situation worth it?"

Finances are truly easy to control and understand. Most decisions we make are based on behavior and very few based on real expenses. And I've been here" but like I said in earlier chapters, I developed systems and strategies to help mitigate empty expenditures. Don't be a slave to debt. Yes, it's extremely difficult not to borrow money in order to make massive purchases. However, make these decisions within reason, according to your income, savings, mindset, and overall financial situation. Remember, it always comes back to behavior and discipline.

Financial Recovery

So you've done shit the bed and accumulated loads of debt. Right now with all your debt, I imagine you're feeling overwhelmed, embarrassed, and like an idiot. This is where the road to financial recovery begins. Understand you are not alone. There are millions and millions of people in debt all over world. But guess what, millions and millions have worked their ass off to get rid of that debt. I was in debt once, and I felt like I had no escape of it. This is where I came with a plan/budget, cut expenses, and got to work paying that shit off. It wasn't easy, but I knew I wanted to change my life, and to do that, I had to become financially sound.

Drinking, abuse, or violence isn't going to help change the situation. It will only make it worse. Nor is taking your life; why people take their life because of financial hardships is beyond me. This just makes you fucking weak. Don't be a bitch.

The road to financial recovery will require patience, discipline, and most importantly time. It will take time. How much time is completely up to you. Also, one thing I notice that helps is sharing your plan with someone. Have a good friend, family member, or perhaps someone in the same situation to keep you or each other accountable. To make change and an impact within your life is easier when you have support.

AUTHOR'S NOTES

Thank you for reading my book. I created it to make you just a little more conscientious about personal finances. This is meant as a baseline, not as the be-all and end-all. As you can imagine, I had fun and an amazing time writing this book. I think this was the first time in my life where I was able to say what I wanted, not having to filter or censor myself.

Like I stated before, I am still an active-duty military. So that means I still need this job for a little bit longer. That means I currently choose to remain anonymous like Satoshi Nakamoto. However, if I sell one hundred thousand copies of this book, I will reveal myself faster than a Kardashian trying to gain attention to stay relevant—not nakedly, of course.

While writing this book, there's a lot of information I learned. However, a lot of things about finances come down to discipline and common sense. Since I've been serving, something like this hasn't been available to the people and is long overdue—a small book of financial guidance where a young man or woman can get some answers, all in one place, while having fun and gaining financial knowledge. Always remember to take the time to continue researching and educating yourself. Semper fi, motherfucker. Just playing, be all that you can be!

www.ingramcontent.com/pod-product-compliance
Lightning Source LLC
Chambersburg PA
CBHW070006180726
48002CB00019B/2575